W9-BPR-426

EPIC
SPORTS
RECORDS

AMAZING
BASEBALL
RECORDS

BY THOM STORDEN

Reading Consultant:
Barbara J. Fox
Professor Emerita
North Carolina State University

CAPSTONE PRESS
a capstone imprint

Blazers Books are published by Capstone Press,
1710 Roe Crest Drive, North Mankato, Minnesota 56003
www.capstonepub.com

Library of Congress Cataloging-in-Publication Data
Storden, Thom.
Amazing baseball records / by Thom Storden.
pages cm.—(Blazers Books. Epic sports records.)
 Includes bibliographical references and index.
Summary: "Provides information on the most stunning records in the sport of professional baseball"
Provided by publisher.
Audience: Age: 8-14.
Audience: Grade: 4 to 6.
ISBN 978-1-4914-0740-0 (Library Binding)
ISBN 978-1-4914-0745-5 (eBook PDF)
Baseball—Records—Juvenile literature. I. Title.
GV877.S7675 2015
796.357—dc23   2014008654.

Editorial Credits
Nate LeBoutillier, editor; Kyle Grenz, designer; Eric Gohl, media researcher;
Kathy McColley, production specialist

Photo Credits
Corbis: Reuters/Sam Mircovich, 7; Dreamstime: Cynthia Farmer, 13, Ronald
Callaghan, 9, 16, 19, Scott Anderson, cover (bottom); Getty Images: 5; Library
of Congress: 10, 15, 23, 29; Newscom: AFP/Scott Rovak, 25, Agence France
Presse/Ted Mathias, 26, EPA/Larry W. Smith, cover (top), Icon SMI/TSN, 20;
Shutterstock: Glen Jones, 1, trekandshoot, 2–3, 30–31, 32
Design Elements: Shuttestock

Records in this book are current through the 2013 season.

Printed in the United States of America in North Mankato, Minnesota..
022015   008786R

TABLE OF CONTENTS

HOW DO WE MEASURE AMAZING?

Baseball is a very **competitive** sport. How do we appreciate great performances yet separate the best from the rest? How do we transform glorious moments in time into golden memories? Keeping records is one way to do it.

competitive—trying to be the best

EPIC//FACT

Yogi Berra of the New York Yankees won 10 World Series titles. Berra's 10 titles are the most of any player in Major League Baseball history.

YOGI BERRA

MOST GRAND SLAMS IN ONE INNING 2

Hitting a **grand slam** home run is like the ultimate baseball party. So imagine how much fun Fernando Tatis had on April 23, 1999. He hit two grand slams in one inning. No one else has ever done that.

OTHER SINGLE-GAME BATTING RECORDS

Hits In a Single Game

9 Johnny **Burnett**, Cleveland Indians, July 10, 1932

Runs Scored in a Game

7 Guy **Hecker**, Louisville Colonels, August 15, 1886

EPIC//FACT

Bill Mueller was a switch hitter. He hit grand slams from both sides of the plate in a game on July 29, 2003.

FERNANDO TATIS

grand slam—a home run with runners on first, second, and third base that scores four runs

switch hitter—batter who is able to hit either left-handed or right-handed

MOST HITS IN A SINGLE SEASON 262

Ichiro Suzuki could probably get base hits in his sleep. The speedy Japanese star came to the United States to play Major League Baseball in 2001. Ichiro got 242 hits in his rookie season. In 2004 he got 262 hits. It was the most hits in a single season.

OTHER SINGLE-SEASON BATTING RECORDS

Highest Batting Average
.440 Hugh **Duffy**, Boston Beaneaters, 1894

Most Triples
36 Chief **Wilson**, Pittsburgh Pirates, 1912

ICHIRO SUZUKI

EPIC//FACT

Ichiro spent his first seven
pro seasons playing in
Japan. He joined the Seattle
Mariners when he was 27.

EPIC//FACT

Ty Cobb was an excellent base stealer.
He stole home plate a record 54 times.

TY COBB

HIGHEST CAREER BATTING AVERAGE .366

Ty Cobb treated baseball like it was war. Pitchers lost many battles with the great hitter. Cobb's career lasted 24 years. His batting average was .366—the highest in the history of pro baseball.

OTHER CAREER BATTING RECORDS

Most Hits
4,256 Pete **Rose**, three teams

Most Stolen Bases
1,406 Ricky **Henderson,** nine teams

OLDEST PITCHER TO WIN A MAJOR LEAGUE GAME 49

Pro baseball is a young man's game. This didn't matter to Jamie Moyer. On May 16, 2012, the Colorado Rockies beat the Arizona Diamondbacks 6-1. The 49-year-old Moyer was the winning pitcher. He became the oldest pitcher to win a game in major league history.

OTHER SINGLE-GAME PITCHING RECORDS

Youngest Pitcher to Win a Game

16	Willie **McGill**, May 8, 1890
	16 years, 5 months, 28 days old

Oldest Pitcher to Throw a No-Hitter

44	Nolan **Ryan**, May 1, 1991
	44 years, 3 months, 1 day old

EPIC//FACT

Jamie Moyer pitched for eight different teams in his pro career.

JAMIE MOYER

MOST WINS IN A SEASON 59

Charlie "Old Hoss" Radbourne was tough. The crafty pitcher played for the Providence Grays in 1884. The Grays only had two main pitchers that season. Then one quit. Old Hoss pitched the final 27 games of the season. He won 59 in all. The Grays won the **pennant**.

OTHER SINGLE-SEASON PITCHING RECORDS

Most Strikeouts

513	Matt **Kilroy** Baltimore Orioles, 1886

Most Saves

62	Francisco **Rodriguez** Los Angeles Angels of Anaheim, 2008

EPIC//FACT

Old Hoss' catchers never wore padding, masks, or even gloves. They caught all his pitches bare-handed.

CHARLIE RADBOURNE

pennant—a triangular flag that symbolizes a championship in baseball

EPIC//FACT

Rivera grew up in Panama and played for the Yankees for 19 seasons.

MOST CAREER SAVES 652

Mariano Rivera was not a pitcher who batters wanted to face in the ninth inning. The tall and slim **relief pitcher** had a blazing fastball and a sharp **cutter**. Rivera retired many batters to finish games. His 652 **saves** set an all-time record.

OTHER CAREER PITCHING RECORDS

Most Wins

511 Cy **Young**, five teams

Most Strikeouts

5,714 Nolan **Ryan**, four teams

relief pitcher–a pitcher who enters the game to replace the previous pitcher

cutter–a fast-moving curveball made famous by Mariano Rivera

save–a statistic in baseball given to a relief pitcher who keeps his team's lead in a close game and finishes the game

MOST POSTSEASON HITS

Batters who collect 200 hits over a full season are considered amazing hitters. As of 2013 Derek Jeter had 200 hits in his **postseason** career alone. No one ever came close to that record before. The 2014 season marked Jeter's 20th season in New York as the Yankees' shortstop.

OTHER POSTSEASON BATTING RECORDS

Most Home Runs

29 Manny **Ramirez**, three teams

Most Runs Batted In

80 Bernie **Williams**, New York Yankees

postseason—the playoffs following the regular season where teams battle for the championship

Derek Jeter won five World Series championships with the Yankees.

EPIC//FACT

Mickey Mantle holds World Series records for home runs, runs scored, runs batted in, walks, and strikeouts.

MOST HOME RUNS IN WORLD SERIES HISTORY 18

The New York Yankees have played in 40 World Series championships. It is not surprising that many of their players hold World Series records. Mickey Mantle was one of the greatest Yankee sluggers. His 18 World Series home runs is a record.

OTHER INDIVIDUAL WORLD SERIES RECORDS

Most Games Played

75 Yogi **Berra**, New York Yankees

Most Pitching Victories

10 Whitey **Ford**, New York Yankees

MOST WORLD SERIES TITLES 27

If you ask people to name just one baseball team, most would say the New York Yankees. The Yankees have been around since 1901. They play in the largest city in the United States. And the Yankees have won 27 championships, the most of any other team by far.

Most World Series Titles

27	New York **Yankees**
11	St. Louis **Cardinals**
9	Philadelphia/Oakland **Athletics**
8	Boston **Red Sox**
7	New York/San Francisco **Giants**

THE 1926 NEW YORK YANKEES

EPIC//FACT

The first World Series was played in 1903. The American League champion Boston Americans defeated the National League champion Pittsburgh Pirates.

MOST WILD PITCHES IN ONE INNING 5

Major league pitchers have great control. They can throw fast or make the ball curve or sink. Rick Ankiel had a day of unusual wildness on October 3, 2000. In one inning, he threw five wild pitches, a major league record.

OTHER EMBARRASSING RECORDS

Most Home Runs Allowed in a **Single Game**

| 7 | Charlie **Sweeney**, St. Louis Maroons, June 12, 1886 |

Most Hits Allowed in a **Single Game**

| 29 | Eddie **Rommel,** Philadelphia Athletics, July 10, 1932 |

wild pitch—a pitch that goes past the catcher and is the fault of the pitcher

RICK
ANKIEL

EPIC//FACT

Rick Ankiel changed positions in 2005.
He went on to play many more games
as an outfielder than as a pitcher.

EPIC//FACT

Cal Ripken's streak of consecutive games played went from May 30, 1982, to September 20, 1998.

MOST CONSECUTIVE GAMES PLAYED
2,632

A good work ethic takes many things. It takes energy, desire, and the ability to show up to work time after time. Cal Ripken Jr. had all of these traits and more. Ripken played a record 2,632 games in a row. In other words, he didn't miss a game in nearly 17 years.

OTHER
CAN YOU
BELIEVE
IT?
RECORDS

Most Complete Games

75 Cy **Young**, three teams

Most Shutouts

110 Walter **Johnson**, Washington Senators

FIRST PLAYER TO REACH 60 HOME RUNS IN A SINGLE SEASON

Babe Ruth was pro baseball's first superstar. People still remember him for his many home runs and big personality. In 1927 Ruth hit 60 home runs for the Yankees. Players have since reached this number in a season. But "The Babe" was the first.

OTHER
CAN YOU
BELIEVE
IT?
RECORDS

Only Pitcher to Record 20 Strikeouts in a Single Game Twice
Roger **Clemens**, Boston Red Sox

Only Catcher to Catch Four No-Hitters
Jason **Varitek**, Boston Red Sox

BABE RUTH

EPIC//FACT

Babe Ruth spent most of his childhood in a reform school, away from his parents.

GLOSSARY

competitive (kum-PET-i-tiv)—trying to be the best

crafty (KRAF-tee)—skilled at tricking other people

cutter (KUT-ur)—a fast-moving curveball made famous by Mariano Rivera

grand slam (GRAND SLAM)—a home run with runners on first, second, and third base that scores four runs

pennant (PEN-unt)—a triangular flag that symbolizes a championship in baseball

postseason (POST-see-zun)—the playoffs following the regular season where teams battle for the championship

relief pitcher (ree-LEEF PICH-ur)—a pitcher who enters the game to replace the previous pitcher

save (SAYV)—a statistic in baseball given to a relief pitcher who keeps his team's lead in a close game and finishes the game

switch hitter (SWICH HIT-ur)—batter who is able to hit either left-handed or right-handed

wild pitch (WIYLD PICH)—pitch that goes past the catcher which is the fault of the pitcher

READ MORE

Howell, Brian. *Amazing Baseball Records.* North Mankato, Minn.: The Childs World, 2013.

Chesterfield, Jack. *400 Amazing Baseball Facts You Never Knew.* New York: Cooperstown Books, 2012.

INTERNET SITES

FactHound offers a safe, fun way to find Internet sites related to this book. All of the sites on FactHound have been researched by our staff.

Here's all you do:

Visit *www.facthound.com*

Type in this code: 9781491407400

Super-cool stuff! Check out projects, games and lots more at **www.capstonekids.com**

INDEX